GOD'S WILL AND OURS

by Roger Hudleston O.S.B.

*All CTS booklets
are published thanks to the
generous support of its Members*

CATHOLIC TRUTH SOCIETY
PUBLISHERS TO THE HOLY SEE

CONTENTS
GOD'S WILL AND OURS

GOD'S WILL AND OURS
IN HAPPINESS

This age of ours, it has been said, is one which longs to be religious: and certainly no one will deny that the men and women of today are interested in religion to a very remarkable degree. Yet we must admit also that it is a time of religious unrest, a time when the spirit of enquiry is so widespread that many are apt to make the fatal mistake of putting search above discovery, of preferring a state of expectation to one of assurance, the search for truth to truth itself; as if a low degree of knowledge were better than a higher one, or a religious system possible without definite, fixed first principles. In consequence many remain always more or less unsatisfied, discontented, restless; they want something, they hardly know what.

Our Search for Happiness

Speaking generally, of course, we all want Happiness; but when we try to define our terms and say what 'Happiness' connotes for us, the real diversity of our aims become apparent.

For some of us Happiness means nothing more than our own personal pleasure, a sense of comfortable well-being, with no anxieties to disturb the surface of our tranquillity.

Pleasures of society, pleasures of eyes, ears, taste, and all the rest, we sample them in turn, according as our taste directs, until at last the exercise grows wearisome, boredom follows eagerness, and pleasure fails to please us any more.

Others again will look to find Happiness in occupation; for them their business or profession is what makes life worth living. Such people will throw themselves into their work with all the energy of their natures, until it comes to be an end in itself - an end so all-absorbing that they lose their sense of proportion, and go through life for years, if not until the end, without realising that, in the stress of work, they have quite forgotten to live at all, in the fuller sense of the term.

And some choose power; physical prowess in sport of war, mental prowess in literature or learning, material power such as wealth - the short cut to surface popularity - or political power with its fascinating influence in affairs local or national, even, it may be, in world politics; power of some kind or other they must have, power to rule others, to make history, to influence the lives of men.

But there is no need to labour the point: it is notorious that each of us does make his choice and that, once made, he strives after his chosen form of happiness with more or less consistency and energy, according to his personal grit and strength of will.

Disillusionment

Now, supposing such a man gain his end, supposing he secure every object of his ambition in this world, what then? Does it follow that he is satisfied, contented, happy? In the majority of cases can we honestly answer 'Yes'? Is it not rather true that, more often than not, his hopes are defeated by his success. The man has got his wish, has tasted, has even sated himself with pleasure, work, or power, with everything that his ambition craved for, only to find that nothing recedes like success, only to discover that his initial choice was a blunder, because the wants of his soul are of another kind.

Sooner or later, for such a person, there comes, there must come disillusionment. "In the hour in which he enters into himself, if he have such an hour, the truth comes back to him with all the force of experience, 'What does it profit a man if he gain the whole world, and suffer the loss of his own soul?" (Ullathorne, *Endowments of Man*) - lost because he has starved it all his life.

Is this too strong, or is it over-coloured, or does our experience of life confirm it? In all honesty, have we not met only too many of whom it is literally true? Some of them perhaps already wholly disillusioned, others half conscious of the coming failure, men and women in whose lives the shades if disappointment have begun to lengthen, who yet are hurrying feverishly onward, seeking to escape from themselves, grasping continually at that which ends in disappointment; seeking, they say, for peace or hope or happiness, yet never understanding that, all the while, the thing they really lack is God.

God, God is what we need. For God alone, and nothing else but God, can fill and satisfy our human nature, fashioned as it is by God in His own image. Without You, O my God, our lives are absolutely doomed to failure, because 'You have made us for Yourself, and our heart knows no rest until it may repose in You' (St Augustine, *Confessions.*)

Key to Our Happiness

And how are we to get to God? How can we rivet the soul to Him so fast that nothing can separate us from Him any more? The answer is very simple: By making His will our own.

To give up our wills to God, and instead to adopt His holy will as our guide in every detail of life; that is the secret of happiness, because it is the only road to that true success which we call everlasting life.

The will of man is the most wonderful force in all creation because it is free. It triumphs over nature, bending the circumstances of life more and more to its own way; until, from being a savage at the mercy of his environment, man becomes a civilised being, controlling Nature ever more and more, and taming all her powers to do his will. And yet, in spite of all its strength, this mighty force, this will of ours is simply so much wasted energy, unless it work in union with the will of God.

'Thy will be done', we pray in every Our Father.

Have you ever noticed the place of that petition in Our Lord's prayer? 'Thy kingdom come, Thy will be done'. Precisely. Christ's kingdom cannot come, His rule cannot be established in our souls, until we submit ourselves to do His holy will. And conversely, once we make our surrender, once we submit our will to His, then His rule begins to be established in the soul. 'The kingdom of God is within you', then and then only, because the essential purpose of that kingdom is to establish Christ's rule in our hearts; and that purpose is only accomplished when our wills are unified with God's will, when deliberately and of set purpose we make His will our own.

This then is the whole essence of religion - to do the will of God. This is the one royal road to success, to that true, everlasting happiness for which mankind is destined. This union of wills is the precise object for which our Father in heaven has placed us in this world, as Jesus Himself has told us, 'I have come, not to do My own will, but the will of Him who sent Me'. And if any one asks why this is so, the reason is evident; because the union of wills is love. Our wills cannot be united to God's will except when we love Him; and if we do really love Him, we find it easy enough to keep His commandments.

'Love God' cries that great lover, St Augustine, 'and do what you will'; because, if you really love God, your will and His are no longer two but one. No matter what He asks of us, it makes no difference now; that such is His will for us is all we need to know. Great things or small, sorrow or joy, wealth or poverty, neglect or recognition, such things as these all cease to matter now, because our scale of values rests on other criteria altogether. For such things are not the material of life's fabric, but merely the dyes which give its threads their colour. The warp and the weft, the dual strands of which man's life is woven, are just God's will and ours.

Co-operation with God: Love

True success in life, then, depends upon the degree in which union can be established between my will and God's. It is a matter of co-operation, of working together with God, and none of us can say he does not know what God would have him do in life, because every duty that comes to him is a direct revelation of God's will in his regard; since, for a Christian, duty is the will of God. To do our duty to God and to our fellow-men - that is the whole purpose of our religious life, the beginning and end of Christianity. For to do our duty means to do the will of God, which is really the same thing as to love Him, since 'love is the fulfiling of the law'.

Nor is it hard to see why this surrender of our wills must, of necessity, bring happiness in its train. Man laughs at that which disappoints his expectations in trifling matters; he weeps over disappointment in the serious, grave, important things of life. Our laughter is born of the surprise, the sudden unexpected incongruity, which rouses no anxiety, no foreboding, no dread of future ills, because it is all over in a moment. While grief and pain, anxiety and unhappiness are caused hardly at all by the shock of the moment, but almost entirely by the expectation of its continuance, the fear of future ills, the prospect of evils long continued and possibly intensified, whose shadows, cast before them, destroy our hopes and darken our lives and so render us unhappy. In a word, unhappiness is due chiefly to fear, and this is so even when the pain is occasioned by some present evil, as, for example, the death of one we love. In such a crisis, the sufferer will reply to our attempts at consolation, 'I cannot face the future, the thought of life without the one I loved so is unbearable'; thus showing that it is the prospect of the future, the feeling that we cannot do without the lost one, it is this fear which is at the back of all our pain.

Love over Fear

Now, 'perfect love casts out fear'; and perfect love, as we have seen above, means perfect resignation to God's holy will; accepting everything He sends as that which He has deliberately chosen for us, and consequently the best thing that can happen in our regard. At present the end is hidden from us, and so we cannot expect to comprehend God's dealings with us. But in every circumstance of life we are in God's hands, nothing can happen to us except by His holy will, and since what God wills is always, must always be the best thing possible for us, there can be no cause for fear, anxiety, foreboding. The future holds nothing we need to be afraid of, if only we hold fast to our great principle of submitting our wills to His in all things. On the contrary, if we can only see it, the loss or suffering or disappointment must be itself the best thing for us at that moment, and so a cause not for regret but for thanksgiving.

It is so. The soul which is really conformed to the holy will of God will thank Him instinctively for everything it receives at His hand. We will look upon disappointment, sorrow, loss, and suffering as gifts of His, no less than joy or pleasure are; we will soon come to count them as incalculably better, because they detach the soul from earth and unite us to God. If then we seek a talisman which will turn our sorrow into joy, which will bring forth happiness out of misery and contentment out of loss, we shall find it in the spirit of thanksgiving.

A Thankful Heart

Only there must be NO exceptions to the rule; no thanking God for some things only and not for others. We must thank God for All things; for pain as well as for pleasure, for permitting us to fail as much as for success, for what He takes away no less than for what He gives. If we can rise to such a degree of resignation, of conformity with God's holy will as this, then all the host of evil is powerless against us; our happiness is beyond its reach, because it is rooted in the will of God - 'God's providence is my inheritance'.

No doubt, in such a matter a this, the only convincing proof is that of personal experience; and so, if any one doubt the truth of what has been said, the answer is, 'Try it and see for yourself'. For the spirit of thanksgiving is nothing else than the habit of thanking God for all things; and, like every other habit, it can be acquired in one way only - namely, by constant repetition of the same simple act. If you really make it a practice to thank God for all things, you will soon begin to find that your view of life and its events will take its colour from your acts of thanksgiving. Very soon depression and gloom will begin to depart, and instead of being a prey to them you will find it possible to 'rejoice in the Lord always', because your spirit is becoming like God's as your will grows more perfectly united to His. In this way your soul begins to acquire true liberty of spirit, a spirit free from fears and unhappiness, because it is transfigured to the likeness of the spirit of God, and 'where the spirit of the Lord is, there is liberty'. And the spirit of the Lord is in them that love Him, it lives in those who seek, always and everywhere, to do in all things His most holy will. 'If you continue in My word', He says, 'then you shall be My disciples indeed; and you shall know the truth, and the truth shall make you free'.

GOD'S WILL AND OURS
IN SUFFERING

In the life of Christ there are two chief elements which surpass all else in importance, His work as Redeemer and His work as Founder of His Kingdom or Church upon earth: and practically every recorded act of His has a bearing upon one or other of these, i.e. is either redemptive or foundational in character.

But His active work is far from being the only aspect of Christ's life which has come down to us. Indeed, it would hardly be too much to say that we know more about the suffering Christ than we do about the working Christ. That, in our concept of Him, His Passion goes for more than His actions. That He is more truly Himself and appeals to us more as 'the Man of sorrows and acquainted with grief', than He does in any other aspect of His endlessly varied character.

We are so well aware of this that we take it as if it were inevitable. 'Jesus Christ, crucified', is so pre-eminently our idea of what the Messiah ought to be, that we are liable to make a mistake about the matter, and look upon Christ's passion and death as a necessary essential, without which His work as Saviour could not have been accomplished. Yet such an assertion cannot be

maintained. Christ might have redeemed us without being
crucified, without dying, without suffering for a single
instant. Once He has become man, every action of His, no
matter how small and insignificant it may appear to the
onlooker, is of infinite value because of His Godhead, and
any one of His acts would suffice to redeem all His
fellow-men, with whom He is now identified because of
His manhood. Clearly then His sufferings were not
essential to His work as Redeemer.

Meaning of Christ's Suffering

Still, while we admit this, our whole heart cries out
against the idea of a non-suffering Saviour. 'Ought not
Christ to have suffered these things and so to enter into
His glory?' The question is His own, and instinctively our
hearts answer 'Yes'. There can be no doubt about it.
Christ's sufferings are an integral part of His life but their
value is not redemptive only, it is foundational as well.
They are there not for our salvation alone, but for our
instruction also as part of His teaching, to show us once
for all the true attitude towards suffering, the attitude
which He Himself adopted and which He expects of His
followers.

And here, for a moment, we may pause to note how, in
this very thing, by His teaching in regard to suffering,
Christ establishes Himself far above all other religious
teachers, and elevates His system to a height undreamed
of before. The problem of pain had faced every pre-

Christian philosophy and system of religion; and, in meeting it, every one of them had fallen either into Pessimism or into Optimism, and so had failed to meet the difficulty. The Pessimist schools, most Oriental in origin, over-burdened with the weight of the problem, had come to see the end of life as trouble and weariness, and taught that man must escape from it into some aloofness, some Nirvana; for life was an evil in itself and must therefore be shunned as evil. The Optimist schools, more typical of Western thought and character, either shutting their eyes to the fact that suffering and sorrow do actually surround us on every side, or else explaining them away, like modern 'Christian Science' does, as a figment of the mind with no reality behind it, had shown themselves incapable of giving a satisfying answer to the problem, and so had demonstrated their inability to help mankind.

But with Christ and with Him alone, the secret of the riddle is found. In Him there is no avoiding of the difficulty nor any foolish denial of its reality. On the contrary He faces it fully and absolutely. He sounds the deepest depths of human sadness and suffering - material and spiritual, bodily and mental, actual, prospective, and retrospective - and He shows us how, if we will only accept them in a spirit of perfect resignation, we may transform our sorrows, by a kind of spiritual alchemy, into the highest, the culminating form of joy.

Nowhere else do we find suffering in such a supreme degree as in the life of Christ. He is the only-begotten of the Father, the Word of God, eternal, immortal, equal with the Father in all perfections, and united to Him in a love so perfect and infinite that it is itself co-equal with both Father and Son, and is personified as the spirit of Love, the Holy Spirit, the third person of the ever blessed Trinity. Considering, then, the perfect love subsisting between God the Father and Jesus the only-begotten Son, we might have expected that His life as God-man would have been one unbroken manifestation of love, in the form of joy, of happiness, of soul-satisfying communion, of perfect bliss. We might have expected the incarnate Son of God to go through the world like some happy prince, scattering a largesse of bliss among His people, sowing happiness, pouring out joy upon the lives of all His fellow-men, simply because He was all joy Himself.

True Nature of Christ

Yet, in reality, we find the exact opposite of this. Christ is 'the Man of sorrows and acquainted with grief', so utterly an outcast that 'the Son of Man has nowhere to lay His head'. He is scarcely born before a deliberate scheme is laid for His assassination, and His active life is displayed by the evangelist against a background of envy, hatred, jealousy, and plots for His destruction. But even stranger and more terrible than all the objective, external suffering which surrounds Him, is His internal, subjective, ever-

present state of sorrow. The shadow of the cross is over
Him from Bethlehem to Golgotha. The betrayal of Judas
is only the last and worst example of the way in which
His chosen ones fail Him again and again. Calvary and
His three hours' agony are but the climax of the treatment
which He receives throughout, for to the end of time He
comes into His own and His own receive Him not. Into
His life of thirty three years are crowded the sorrows of
all ages, and in the agony in Gethsemane He foresees and
undergoes the concentrated malice and hatred of every
affront and rejection, of every outrage, sin, and act of
treachery which mankind has ever committed and ever
will commit until the end.

All this, far from being an exaggeration, is but the
merest outline of the reality, an understatement, utterly
inadequate to the truth. For the more we study the life of
Jesus and the more intimately we search into its secrets,
the stronger grow its contrast and its paradox. Nowhere
else in human experience do we find such height and
depth, such blinding light, and such unfathomed
darkness, as we find when we draw near to Him.

No wonder His human soul cries out in agony against
the treatment which the Son received from the Father!
For the love of God is a consuming fire, incredibly more
jealous, more exacting, more consuming - often, it seems
to us, more cruel - than any passion that is known to our
poor, narrow, selfish human hearts. 'God is love' most
emphatically does not mean 'God is good-nature', 'God

is easy-goingness', 'God is indulgence'. On the contrary, the touch of His fondest caress may burn the soul like a flame. 'Whoever He loves, He chastises and scourges every son whom He accepts'. 'His fan is in His hand, and He will truly purge His floor', and not until the flail has threshed away the utmost shred of chaff will He gather the wheat into His storehouse.

Christ suffered, then, to a degree of which we can form no adequate conception, and He did so to manifest to us the absolute necessity of suffering. And we too must suffer in our turn, so that we may learn to love God only, for in His love alone is our eternal life. 'How hard it is for a rich man to enter into the kingdom of heaven'. Why so? Because it is just earthly riches - by which is meant earthly happiness and enjoyment, the love of things earthly - which make the love of God most difficult, indeed, impossible for us. There is no road to God except by absolute, deliberate self-surrender; the more He strikes us, the more we must learn to love Him and to understand.

To the worldly, to the shallow-hearted, such a theory of life may seem too terrible. 'What a wretched existence', they will say, 'what a misery is Christian life, if what you say be true!'

Secret of True Joy

But it is not so: we Catholics at any rate, can say no such thing. For is there one of us who does not know that suffering and sorrow can retain their bitterness only so long as we rebel and fight against them? The moment we resign ourselves to them and cease to struggle, the moment we really accept them as being God's will in our regard, and therefore the best possible thing in the world for us, at that moment the cloud is lifted and our sorrow is turned into joy.

At the end of His agony in the garden, when Jesus spoke the words 'Thy will be done', angels came down and ministered to Him. So with us, the secret of true joy is resignation, accepting all our sorrow and suffering as God's holy will, and humbly giving up our wills to Him. Love is the only perfect happiness, and love is nothing else but self-surrender, giving up heart and will and all our being to Him who only loves us perfectly. And, of necessity, joy must follow in the train of love. For the source of all sorrow, the final cause of all suffering, is simply fear; and, once the total surrender to God's will is made, fear ceases to be possible for us any longer, since 'perfect love casts out fear'.

'Thy will be done', that is the password to the Kingdom. For this self-surrender is the habitual attitude of mind or, if you will, the spirit of the sons of God. And without it we simply cannot be members of His kingdom, seeing that its whole purpose, the very reason for its existence, is to unify our wills with God's will, so that our hearts, our minds, and our whole lives may be united perfectly to Him.

Give, in Self-Surrender

If we can only bring ourselves to make the venture - to give, give, give ourselves and all that we are to God - then in return we gain the prize of prizes, the gift of God, which is God Himself, no less. Undoubtedly 'the distinctive religious act is, as such, an unconditional surrender. Nowhere in life can we both give and keep at the same time, and least of all here, at life's deepest sources' *(Von Hugel, The Mystical Element of Religion).*

'Remember', says St Paul, 'that word of the Master, how He said, 'It is more blessed to give than to receive' '; and again, 'He that loses his life for My sake shall find it'. It is so; Christ has taught us the truth of His words by His example, showing us once for all how 'greater love has no man than this, that a man lay down his life for his friend'. 'I am come that they may have life, and that they may have it more abundantly'. Now life is love, nothing else; and it is only when we lay down our lives for God, when we cease to live for self, and resign ourselves simply and absolutely to the will of the divine lover that by losing the lesser life we gain the life more abundant, the life divine which Jesus came to give us.

Let us make no mistake about it. 'Jesus Christ, crucified' is the gospel which Christ's Church is set to preach. Hence the crucifix is the central object on her altars, and the mystical death of Jesus in the Mass is her supreme religious act, the heart from which her very life pulsates.

So, in like manner, among her children, those millions of souls who make up the Church, or mystical body of Christ, it is the suffering members who are nearest to the inmost heart of things, because it is theirs to follow most intimately in His footsteps, to 'bear in' their 'body the marks of the Lord Jesus', the royal sign-manual of their crucified King. For this reason St Paul does not hesitate to write, 'I fill up that which is wanting in the sufferings of Christ', words which at first sight seem almost too astonishing to be taken literally. Yet who can doubt that the Apostle meant them to be so taken? Christ's earthly life is over, His direct personal sufferings ceased when He died upon the cross; but He has left suffering as a legacy, an heirloom to those who call themselves by His name. No true Christian, no follower of Christ, who has counted the cost of his profession, can ever complain if he be asked to suffer. 'The servant is not greater than his Lord', and what our King saw best to undergo, that same, beyond all question, it is best for us to undergo as well.

Suffering of the Elect

We need not ask ourselves why it is that some suffer intensely for years, possibly for their whole lives, while others go through life with little or none of it. It would be as much use to ask why some members of the human body are active and some passive, why some are external and some internal, some designed for giving and some for receiving. The simple fact is that the body would not be complete without organs of such diverse character; and similarly Christ's mystical body, the Church, must have its suffering members, just as it has its active members and its contemplative ones, in order that it may be a complete body, not a mere torso.

But what if our individual lot be cast in such ways of pain? If sickness, sorrow, desolation, loss, are the bread of life to us, or the setting in which our lot is cast, what then? Why, then let us take heart and bear our sorrows proudly, for such as these are indeed the chosen ones of Jesus, His nearest and dearest, knit unto Him by the most intimate of all bonds, the sympathy that comes of perfect understanding, the fellow-feeling which unites all those who share life's deepest experiences together. 'The lot is fallen unto me in a fair ground; lo, I have a goodly heritage', for these are they who 'fill up that which is wanting in the sufferings of Christ'. It is theirs to bear His cross with Him to Calvary, to 'show forth the Lord's death until He come', since, by their vicarious suffering, they carry on His work until the end.

Of all their grief and pain nothing shall be lost; though not until the books are opened and the secrets of all hearts revealed, shall any know how great a work these unknown, silent heroes have achieved. How in their lonely outposts and secret strongholds they have kept watch and ward over the weak ones of the flock, or fought and won the battles of the Lord. Such valiant souls know well 'that word of the Master, how He said, 'It is more blessed to give than to receive'.' As St Teresa, their spokesman, has put it, they ask 'either to die, or to suffer'. For they, the bearers of Christ's fiery cross, have read the message its fierce light reveals; and since, through God's great love, they may 'die daily', without their sufferings life would not be worth living.

'... It seems to me there is nothing worth living for but this (viz. to suffer), and suffering is what I most heartily pray to God for. I say to Him sometimes, with my whole heart: 'O Lord, either to die or to suffer! I ask of Thee nothing else for myself'. It is a comfort to me to hear the clock strike, because I seem to have come a little nearer to the vision of God, in that another hour of my life has passed away'. (St Teresa, *Life*)

GOD'S WILL AND OURS
IN DEATH

It is common psychology that men are apt to be impressed most easily by the unknown. So one English philosopher writes, 'Men fear death as children fear to go into the dark'. Indeed, for many Death is the king of terrors precisely because of the endless possibilities which it holds, and such men, ostrich-like, will refuse to face it or give it a thought if they can help; as if, by shutting their eyes to the fact of Death and all it must and ought to mean to us, they were somehow screening themselves from it or delaying its approach.

Needless to say, this is not the attitude of the Catholic Church. On the contrary, there is scarcely a feature of human experience on which she insists so constantly as Death. Every one of her liturgical offices concludes with a prayer for the faithful departed; every Mass has its memento of the blessed dead. We cannot say a 'Hail Mary' without calling to mind the hour of our death - as if to keep us in memory of the words spoken by God to our first parents when they fell from grace, and renewed each Lent as the ashes are sprinkled on our heads, 'Remember, O man, that you are dust, and into dust you shall return'.

Familiarity with Death, then, is a characteristic of the Catholic spirit. Indeed, it would hardly be too much to say that its presence in the mind is a test of the true child of the Church; for, as St Benedict reminds us in his famous chapter on the Instruments of Good Works, 'To keep Death every day before our eyes' is the way a Christian ought to live.

What then is Death?

For the absolute materialist - if any such really exist today - Death is extinction, annihilation, the end of personal existence. And this is reason enough why he should shun the thought of it, if he really holds that life ceases altogether then and naught remains but a corpse doomed to speedy disintegration; because the life, the soul, has come to an end, like the flame of a burnt-out candle.

Scarcely less depressing is the neo-pagan view of Death put forward so commonly by the poetic writers of recent times. For them Death is a sleep, an endless rest for tired mortals, who linger on in a dim twilight existence, not unlike that of the shades in the classical Hades - 'by the banks of a dreamy river, 'mid poppies and asphodels' - where pale, thin ghosts drift softly by, borne on the pinions of oblivion. For such views of Death as these the Catholic Church has frankly no use.

In her eyes, Death is simply an episode in the life of man, a phase in his development which, although unique in some respects like many another phase of life is, must nevertheless be recognised as merely a part of the natural process through which every individual human being must go to reach the fullness of the stature which his Creator has designed for him. It has, however, one peculiarity distinguishing it from all other stages of natural human development, namely, that while all the other steps in that process are inevitable, owing to the nature man's body and soul have received from the Creator, Death was not always so. Alone among the number, Death has been a step in human development through the action of man himself. Had he perfectly obeyed God's law he would never have been called upon to die. But, seeing he did thus disobey, his sin inevitably brought punishment in its train, and that punishment is Death. Thus Death is simply the official penalty due to sin, for it is sin, and nothing else, which has brought Death into the cycle of man's experience: 'by one man sin entered into this world, and by sin death: and so death passed upon all men'; 'the wages of sin is Death'; 'in Adam all die'; and as children of Adam we all share in the legacy of woe which his primal act of disobedience has entailed upon his children to the end.

Finality of Death

And this punishment is Death - that is, the separation of man's soul and body; nor is it difficult to see why the

penalty should take this form. Here, in this life, we are
compassed about continually with material things. On
every side, at every moment, whatever our state of mind
or feeling, the external world is in touch with us, and our
five senses are ever greedily at work, sampling and
tasting it, establishing relations, points of union, bonds of
sympathy between us and the things of this world. If this
world were the only one and material good, the only kind
of which man was capable, this piling up of sense-
connections with the material universe would be wholly
desirable. But since this is not so, since all that is best and
noblest in man is spiritual rather than material, is of the
soul rather than of the body, this over-insistence of sense-
perception and surface knowledge is only too liable to do
harm, to fetter the soul, to imprison the spirit in the flesh,
until its chief if not its only use is merely to sing sweet
songs to the senses and give an intellectual relish to what
would otherwise be a wholly animal happiness.

　　At Death all this ceases. The five senses collapse and
fall with the failure of the body and cease to tell us
anything more. So Death is the great reducer. More than
anything else it tends to bring things down to their lowest
terms and make them appear at their true value, their
eternal value - the value they have in comparison with
God and the things of God - instead of at the fictitious
values which we choose to give them in the rag-market of
our daily life. Herein is the importance of making Death a
subject of meditation, of the caution 'to keep Death every

day before our eyes'. For Death shows us, as nothing else can do, the utter folly of those who live as if this life on earth were all; who are 'fools' in the strict meaning of the word. For a fool is one who does not take things at their true worth, but instead makes nought of that which is of value and gives to trifles an imaginary importance - like children in a game, who make pretence that stones are bread, or shells are merchandise, or counters money, and keep it up until their bedtime comes, when toys are put away and such pretences end.

Foolish to Ignore Death

Yet how many such fools there are on earth today! Is it not simply folly for us to dedicate our life to things of earth alone, to pleasure, money, position, influence, forgetting that each of us possesses an immortal soul, fashioned by God with a capacity and a desire for the infinite - that is, for union with God Himself? Certainly we shall do well to keep Death every day before our eyes if doing so makes us live in the presence of God, in the light of His truth, in the remembrance of His judgment to come.

There is an old prayer, popular many years ago, which contains this petition: 'Grant us, O Lord, to live this day as we shall wish that we had lived, when we stand before your judgment seat'. Why should we ask this? Surely because it is then, when Death has cut us off from all things visible, from everything that is attractive to the senses, that we shall understand - when the knowledge is too late to be of use - that God is the only thing which matters, and that if we are living for anything else but God, we are simply wasting our time. It is so. Outside of God, everything else is a trifle endowed with fancied value, a playing at life, a pretence of reality where none is.

Gift of Death

Now for each of us the time of Death is fixed and certain. At this moment God knows the day, the hour, the minute when every one now alive will die. What we must do is to look forward, not to shut our eyes. To face Death and accustom ourselves to the thought of its coming, to prepare or it, lest our end take us by surprise. Most of all we must school ourselves to recognise that the hour of Death is our supreme and final opportunity, the last great chance we shall have; so that in it we can and ought to surrender ourselves, to give ourselves up to God with perfect trust and love and confidence, deliberately yielding up our lives into His hands, laying down our wills in absolute submission to His holy will, and accepting His decree as the best thing possible for us, because that moment is the one which He has chosen as our last.

No doubt, if a man has deliberately shut his eyes to the inevitable and refused to face the thought of Death, such calm submission will be impossible to him, but it does not present any great difficulty to those who have looked forward to Death deliberately and have made it their business to prepare for it. 'He that loves his life shall lose it, and he that hates his life in this world keeps it until life eternal'; for, of course, this preparation is not a matter of meditation only. On the contrary, our preparation for Death should enter into and modify every part of our life, in the same insistent manner that systematic training does in the life of an athlete. There is no need here to go into details, it is enough to say that as the life has been so will the death be. For just as no one becomes wholly depraved all at once, so no one can meet Death with true submission if he put off trying to do God's holy will until the hour when his own freedom of will is passing from him forever.

After all, why should it be so hard for us to yield, why should we be so loth to go to God? For us Christians, Death is not, as it is to the materialist or the semi-pagan, an end; it is rather a beginning. For what is life but one long series of awakenings? At birth we are all unconscious of our surroundings. Then gradually consciousness awakens in us. We are existing, and all around us are thousands of things, each one of them different from us and from each other, and all so many possibilities for our use and enjoyment. At first each makes himself the centre of his tiny world; for children are admittedly self-centred. Then the borders expand and childhood dies out of us as knowledge widens. We find out endless things, some pleasant, some unpleasant: material things, food, toys, games, animals; things intellectual, books, studies, art, and science. We discover new worlds unguessed at hitherto, a universe of thoughts and schemes, shadow and light, sight and sound, sunset and storm, creative power in sculpture, colour, language; the magic of harmony, the sense of humour, the infinite variety and charm of human intercourse. And then, perhaps, if we are lucky, we learn the great truth that love is the only thing which satisfies, and so we come to love mankind, made in God's image, and last of all we find the love of God.

Death a beginning for Christians

And, after all these new awakenings, each of which was more or less a death to earlier interests, may we not hope that Death, when it arrives, will be nothing else except the last, most wonderful awakening? For how can it be anything except the supreme blessing if it admits us to the presence of God? 'We see now as through a glass in a dark manner, but then face to face. Now I know in part, but then I shall know even as I am known'.

Yes, Death is the only event our future holds about whose coming we can be absolutely certain, and if we will but make it so, as it is in our power to do, Death will be for us not an end, but rather a beginning; not so much a fresh start in living, but the real thing for the first time. In this life, so fettered is the soul by the body that we hardly do more than play at being free, living creatures. Once past death we have the reality, the true life of freedom; for

GOD'S WILL AND OURS

Death is the birthday of the soul on which we may pass from the shadows and the semblance to the truth.

Until we can bear to face the thought of Death we have scarcely started to be Christians; for our religion, our Christianity is little better than superstition - unless it leads us to put trust in Jesus. But if we have attained a real love for Christ, then the prospect of Death becomes for us one not of fear, in spite of its uncertainty, but one of trustful confidence. For as our bodily senses fail and those five lamps, whereby we gaze upon the world, give out and darken one by one, then it is that we are left alone, alone with Jesus, our best of friends, protectors, comforters, who loved us so dearly that He laid down His life for us, and now is asking us to yield up our lives to Him.

If then a soul has made God's holy will its guide through life, if it has tried, in spite of all its weakness to unify its poor, feeble human will with the perfect, never-changing will of God, it need not fear the passage through the gate of Death, for here, as everywhere, it knows the password:

'Thy will be done'.

'Pass friend', the sentry answers.

And so instead of the grisly horror that we shunned, Death proves to be the smiling porter of eternity; and we, instead of shrinking from His presence, go forth, in trust, happily to meet Him'.

THE CTS

We hope you have enjoyed reading this booklet. If you would like to read more of our booklets or find out more about CTS - Why not do one of the following?

1. Join our Readers CLUB.

We will send you a copy of every new booklet we publish, - through the post to your address. You'll get 20% off the price too.

2. Support our publishing work.

Become a CTS MEMBER for just £15 a year. We'll send you our Members Newsletters, Catalogues, keeping you up to date with our work.

3. Get our Information Pack.

Find out more about CTS, our publications, our work, and the many ways you can participate - such as opening a CTS Bookstall.

Call us now on 0171 640 0042 or return this form to us at CTS, 40-46 Harleyford Road, Vauxhall, London SE11 5AY (Fax 0171 640 0046 Email:ctspublishers@mcmail.com)

❏ I would like to join the CTS Readers CLUB

❏ I would like to support CTS as a MEMBER.
I enclose payment of my first annual subscription (payable to the CTS) for £15 (suggested) or £............ (other amount)

❏ Please send me a CTS Information Pack

Name:..

Address: ....

....

....

Post Code: .... Phone: ....

Registered charity no.218951. Registered in England as a company limited by guarantee no.57374